The Transparent Body

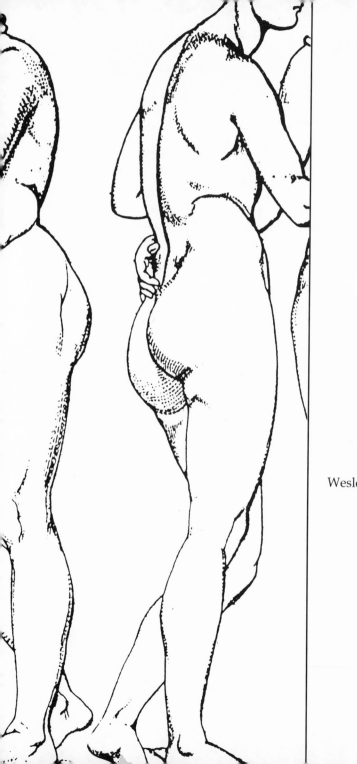

Wesleyan New Poets

The
Transparent
Body

Lisa Bernstein

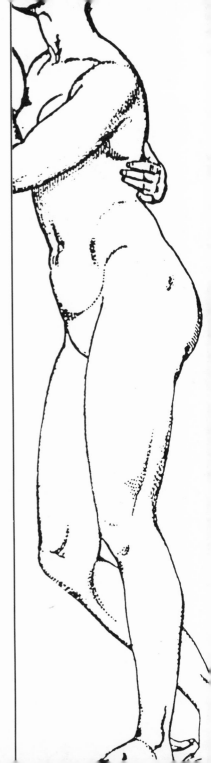

 Wesleyan University Press
Middletown, Connecticut

Grateful acknowledgment is made to the following magazines and anthologies, which first published some of the poems in this book: *Alcatraz, Ally, Antaeus, Calyx, City Lights Review, Five Fingers Review, Kalliope, Kayak, Men & Women: Together & Alone, Mirage, Pulpsmith,* and *Yellow Silk.* And sincere thanks to all who gave this collection their criticism and support, especially Lynn Luria-Sukenick, Kim Addonizio, and Rich Yurman.

All inquiries and permissions requests should be addressed to the Publisher, Wesleyan University Press, 110 Mt. Vernon Street, Middletown, Connecticut 06457

Library of Congress Cataloging-in-Publication Data

Bernstein, Lisa.
   The transparent body/Lisa Bernstein.—1st ed.
      p.   cm. — (Wesleyan new poets)
   ISBN 0 - 8195 - 2162 - 0
   ISBN 0 - 8195 - 1163 - 3 (pbk.)
   I. Title. II. Series.
PS3552.E7364T7 1989
811'. 54 — dc19   88 - 10656
                  CIP

Manufactured in the United States of America

First Edition

Wesleyan New Poets

Contents

I

II

III

I

The Sentence

Green thread
is stitched in my hem,
small marks in
white linen and
after each one
like an eyelash a
longer stitch.
A camera latches
like a door and opens
when I turn
around on the lawn so
the tops of my legs show
and he says Ready?

Alone in my
room I look at
brown knotholes and
hope they don't
start to look like faces.
Another girl
with no body or
different thoughts than
mine but she is
a different girl, a
place in the air
shaken. The air molecules
are silver, and she is them
dancing.
She is a door left open.

If she had legs
someone would have
sewn them together.
I don't know if

there would be
blood-marks. Not
like hairs you
can see. When the
cupboard door
closes, the hairs and
darkness in there.
There is an in-there
even if you can't
say what happened.

When I listen to
my father I am
very good at
finishing his
sentence if he
wants me to finish it.
If he doesn't I can't
sew this girl's legs shut like she
needs me to.
Lips are stitched quiet.
No one touches her
but they think it
and it doesn't have words
so it didn't happen.
The room is a closed
cupboard and the dust is
in the back of my throat
shutting it.
If I talk and someone
hears me, will they know
the dust is in there?

4

Spider in the corner
don't go to sleep.
How did you
sew those strands
together? When I know
I will be crying.
The words will be the
ones I'm saying.
See the molecules
of shaking air.
A door open.
The different girl
for me to walk through.

A Girl

had a mouse's mouth,
little, no whiskers.

She bathed her feet—
small birds,
rubbed to a robin's red.

Her cheek
was flour and yellow egg,
patted and baked
like cake, her mama said.

I want a baby girl
to coo in my arms
and suck, the girl said,
to cook pots of stew
for her, and toss her under the bed.

A house of crayons,
aquamarine and orchid.
I want a crown of feathers
on my head.

The road to my house
is made of fingers and lips,
she said,
when she and her mommy
kissed.

Jumping

My mother interrupts, extends her hand, offers a bowl of polished apples.

I am still jumping. Blue shadows leap and fall on the walls. My feet bounce on the waxed linoleum. I can see the rope's ellipse as it evades strangulation, each time, sideways, losing its shadow on the wall, then skipping white and taut under my feet.

Stripe of shadow. Skitter against floor. Grimy rope in my small palms. The frightening silence.

Lately, every evening, my skirt lapping my thighs and flouncing away, I want my mother to interrupt again, lips parted, brown eyes brimming, to extend that bowl wobbling with mountainous apples.

How can I stop? I can crouch, the knobby knees rising up, mountainous. A bright rope drifts beyond my window. The willows toss at its frayed light.

The solid floor refuses each time I hit. For an instant, the enlarging air. Inhale. Then I drive down, testing this hardness against my toes, tendons, thighs, shoulders like hills rising through breezes, cheeks red as apples pulled down and reappearing, unpicked, on this springing branch.

This season, wrenched up and never quite rooting, the green tips sway, hooking the light, gorgeously reused.

My mother is lonely in the abandoned room, offering apples, shining hair fastened back—

Moon, sweep up past my roof. I am jumping here still. Yet I'd lose track if I could. Blink. In the stillness, leaves scratch the walls. I'd see the arm draw back.

The Family Rage

Her chalk feet in black peat,
fingers tracing
the line of her neck, her eye sockets
ground empty.
The figure walked through the garden,
head like fennel on fire, each shake
scratching a streak into the dusk.

The blue veins not painted
down her wrist and forearm. She never
thought of severing her vessels.
This evening she imagined holding a knife,
its blade pressed inside the
wooden handle in her grip
as safe as the bones in her flesh.

She tramped past the low white wall
by the willows. A little girl
was looking out the window. "Someone
is burning leaves in the yard,"
the girl thought. Her mother stared out
from upstairs at a gray scrap of cloth
caught on a branch.

The figure could not speak to either. She barely
saw the father, his saxophone swinging
up and down behind the brown glass.
The cold lay like a coin on her tongue.
A metallic aftertaste
rinsed their mouths. Tomorrow
the little girl's throat will swell shut.
The mother will stand over her bed,
one hand pressing in the fever.

The Seamstress

Who gave me this white dress?
I've lost my own head—
I wove it with spindles
and sharp, silky thread.

Whose fingers have vanished?
Not mine, not mine.
I trundle the stockings,
the lace in its line.

Who made me suspicious?
I change cloth all day
from linen to wool
until the threads fray.

Whose mother, whose daughter,
what woman's ghost?
I hear singing, a lace wind,
in the rooms of my house.

On my sofa I'll sew her
a cloth of her song
which I bought with my fingers,
I wove and I wore.

I'll spin her a silk net
that I've spun before
of her voice, her snippings,
her lace on my floor.

The rose on the doily
is the print of my thumb,
my flashing needle
the shape of the thorn.

And my lips humming
on the warp of the loom
draw my song down in the shuttle:
soon, soon, soon, soon.

Foraging

I find a nectarine cut open on the kitchen table, the pocked pit in one half, the stringy red hollow beside it. I eat the ripe fruit, juice dripping from my fingers, then hold in my palm what remains, unmistakable, dry. Once it rounded the flesh like pregnancy. Now it must show itself, a mouth sewn shut, nothing inside.

A windowsill. A sly apricot pit lies there in the sun. Someone has polished it. I wish I could rest there like that, my caretaker at the table reading. I'd wait on the white-painted wood while she smacked her lips in unashamed pleasure, sucked the juice from a plum. Parched, I'd keep still. Her breathing could sweep me outside.

Instead I stand beside the mahogany table, loosening my string bag. Cherries tumble onto dark wood. I wash them; my tongue toys with a pit. My mother looks up from her plate, stares at my red handful. The pit almost slips between my fingers. I hold the chewed cherry meat in my mouth.

She keeps eating, shifts her gaze past me out the window. An old woman bends by the peach tree, her face pressed like a leaf. She holds an empty wooden bowl. The wind flattens her print dress against her hips. My mother chews faster as my grandmother's elbows lift and fall, white wings. We both watch her forage, hidden in yellow grass, reappearing, the bowl an oval shadow at her side.

Reaching for the Branch

My mother's arm extends and pulls the shade down halfway. Leaves toss at the window, fragrant masses of flattened hands, slicing the breeze.

Below, the hot path. Bruised knees. Legs nicked by collisions with sharp-edged tables and balconies now take me into the orchard.

I can't climb without a ladder. My bare toes cling to the rungs. I am blind from the waist up, and this land like a hot cut-open pie stretches below.

The tree waves jagged around me, a ferocious clatter. Burnt from waiting. What dangles from the branch, easy to pick? I reach for the limb.

My fingers stretch, the veins of my hands green stems: and cannot pick.

My mother is masked by a yellow shade from the waist up. Her wide lap, enfolded by a green dress, shifts behind glass. Her fingers curl as if gripping a rolling pin, flatten as if rolling out dough. She is promising a fruit pie that will fill us both.

Inhaling peat moss and rotten apricots, I see her veins straining and blueing her skin. Can't look at her or my own straight chest, its clinging sweat. Only these toes working down the rungs.

Beyond here is a road, a school. Tingling begins between shoulders and neck. The flat leaves glint behind me, different from the limb. My neck extends. Sun burnishes my head. I walk down the gravel lane. Behind me a crown of willows bends down, too late.

Two Nudes

I wait with you.
Green watercolor hills,
wheat sheaves soft
and amber as my breasts.
Mother, why won't you look
at me? From the corner of my eye, I'm
loving you. A violet paintbrush
outlined my shoulders, ribs, waist,
the barest drawing
of your pigmented full body.
Pinched red scar crossing your belly,
puckered brown nipples—

All afternoon you watch the fields,
my fingers gripped
in yours, hidden
between your thigh and mine.
The plane of your cheek, the sunlight
wavering across the patch of dust
where the hens scratch.
A mahogany man shifts
behind the hedge, a swatch of burnt umber
stretching all the way through him,
from your dimpled leg to the oaks
lining the road. Mother,
do you see him waiting for me
to leave you? The sour heat
slopes between our shoulders.
The lopsided eggs, brown and white,
fill the bin—

There, watch the hawk glide
through two gold and green trees!
The russet hen trots into the weeds, quiet

as we are. His wings shadow
her back. Could I walk away and
stroke her feathers as she nestles?
You fix your gaze on the man
I'd have to pass, imagining my wrist,
slim and white, wrenched through
the criss-crossed twigs — and I can't
say a word. My smile is a red
half-circle, like the scar
I marked you with at birth.

But you don't turn to see. My thighs
an unfinished triangle. I'm too
young, too old. Soon the wet crimson
will streak the hen's middle,
her feathers matted, her plump body still
under the rising hawk. Mother
do you see the day
when I scoop her from the weeds
and hold her to my chest,
my back to you?

Uncovered Canyon

A small girl
lies on a sofa, someone's fingers
inside her.
Years after, she rises
wearing her limbs, retrieved
from the leaf gulch, bronzed and wavering.
The others lie under the picnic table,
white ovals of food
in the wooden bowls and inside their skins.
A trail of rice on the ground
leads to a scrim of sunlight and redwood needles
which divides the eaters from the corpses.
A knothole a fist is
thrust into. The uterus matted with blood
seen in the underpants.
Cramping:
the fist
dissolving from inside.

In the canyon the dog barks
and the buzz saw.
The trunk is slashed, termites,
and no matter how many steps are taken
the hill is piled all over with mulch.
My foot moves the leaves from the
coyote's gashed throat, her
brown eyes and no moisture
like them in the night sky.
Look up, exhale. Still
she's lying there.
The one trail back out
leads past the other bodies, fingers
curling onto air.
No words.

The black sheen of my back
is like a slick of menses
glimpsed by the one who is past bleeding.
Her arm lifts across
what she sees of the night.
The stars
too bright to blot out.

Jumping Rope in the Yard

The neighbor's dog leaps for the fence, his chain
rattles as it drags him back.
I swing the rope.
His yelp loosens through the night
and I jump over it,
the bones of my feet
thudding, lifting off.

The plums sway
in the dark, smooth
as my father's brow above my pillow
hiding the stars when I knew they'd collapse.
He recited 2 times 6,
divided by 3, square root of,
plus itself. When we arrived at 4
hysterical outer space resolved
into a constellation, a gleaming number
we silently summed.

Plum petals drift past,
covering the cement.
I rise, counting each time
my twine parabola slashes the stars.
The rope collapses.
No equation encloses us
but my two jumping feet.
I call out for the past
and slash through it, my breath
misting the margin between leash and star.
Soon I lose track.
The spacious hush before sleep
blossoms from the lights.
I let go.

Gravity

The bee circles
my orange sweater,
the tiny moth
fixes on my hair.
All things sing
with striped bristling fur
and wings, as they grip
and eat.

A stripe of cloud
drifts its shadow
across my thigh.
Even the earth strains each month,
north and south toward the moon,
the jutting rocks, leaves,
everything fixed but the tides.
They breathe and slide,
clam holes are ringed with crystal,
uncovered again to light.

Is this how to order my life?
Pulling in, spitting back salt,
etching designs on quartz?
Even Jupiter moves to its moons
flipping by in the hot sky.
Even Pluto, once the heart
of a broken star, has fallen in
with the sun, and spins.

Pulling each other around
and around, in darkness,
in fire, the molten rock
and the moth hold on,
circling light.

II

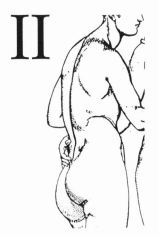

Seashore

I lower my face
between his legs, nuzzling
the reddish cloud of hair
rising from his balls.
They drift, delicately ridged,
skin rosy and taut, as I tongue
a long vein in his cock, and clasp
the smooth slit head until it pops from my
fingers. I glimpse
his white brow, an unfurling wave.

(And remember salt spray in the face of a
ten-year-old girl, who slaps the wet sand
laughing as the tide drifts back
like a blanket, thinking that everyone on the beach
can see her half-naked, belly down
in the warm shallows
that sway under her thighs.)

Pale as sand, his temple
where a green vein pulses,
each inhalation
a withdrawing wave, his sigh repeating
down the beach until it strums
my cheeks, and the sunlit froth
seeps through my fingers.
His eyes open: cirrus-streaked sky
shadowed with the girl's face.
Her smile fills the horizon,
his hand cupping her cheeks,
pulling us both to his lips.

Eating the Heart

In my embroidered slippers,
I sit at the table
peeling the artichoke leaf
by leaf, scraping off the pulp
with my teeth. My ladylike
ankles cross. I uncover
the hairy pedestal
but I can't slice it through
without gouging the tenderest part.

Then you sit down. Your wishful glance
rests on the buttered stem
slick between my finger and thumb.
You want to help me pare away
the prickly meat, but you are not
my father, and not a child anymore
I must use my knife.
I carve out the limp
ivory hairs, and bite into
the gray heart.

A wisp of it sticks in my throat.
The splintered points of the leaves
lodge in my fingertips.
Half the meat crumbles
on my plate. Too late for your
expertise, only your exhaustion
waits, breathing
against my tendriled neck.
I retreat
from your efficient rinsing,
as your agile fingers pick off

what I've stubbornly scarred—
the secret delicacy I won't
take whole from your knife
or give whole to you.

Wedding Feast

Breezes swept us back
from the shore. Chill uncles
circled the bourbon.
The two men waited, smoothing their chests
as straight as tables. Against his white linen
she lay her head
and bit into the ripe, purple plum
I could not share with her,
the marriage kiss.

Later she gave me what other guests
rolled in their palms,
the almond eggs,
discreetly ribboned and flowering.
I ate them, and tied the paper blooms
to my wrist. The bride hovered
among the eaters, her basket empty.
Her corsage's pink heart
gave up its perfume.

Through the glass doors I could see gulls
wheeling and diving. Waves unfurled
like a wedding dress on the sand,
gradually vanishing. At dusk
she kissed my cheek, and I turned back
to the best man, holding between my finger and thumb
the miniature paper bouquet. I hold onto it still

in the mirror, the silver water
we walked from, her arms brown as cake
spreckled with nutmeg, her teeth the silk icing
slick to my tongue. I wait
to step through this glass door with her,
to burst into blossom
with these papery flowers.

The Woman Between Us

She waits, taut as a net,
for me to fall from him,
a torn sail. As if spread on the water,
blanking out, I glimpse
my long brown hair sweeping his shoulder
and dizzy with sunlight
I'm washed back to his shore.
He doesn't see her shape appearing,
a paper lantern outlined
by twine, the curve of her breasts
precise as ink, the down of her belly
brushstrokes of a name.
He reaches for me but her
milky buttocks slope between us,
her body a flicker of lace
flattening as our hips meet
and unfurling as we slip apart.
I cling to his hard, curved chest,
my fingers caught in his red-gold hair,
bite his neck and the flesh
above his ribs. All his weight
can't erase her sheen
from my skin. Open-mouthed,
silent as she is silent,
inhaling with her, exhaling
with him, I cry out—
a white gown unraveling
around me, her heat. We are alone
with her absence. He sees me
transparent, the length of my body
lit up with loving him and
trying to keep her in sight.
He watches me looking
and doesn't look away.

2

"I was spilled from the glass
you kept by the bed.
Like a man at a drying river
he lapped me up. And offers you
salty mouthfuls from his body,
muscle to lean your cheek against.
His fine hairs like meadow weed
stiffen in the dusk.
His flesh is packed gold clay
and he wants you to draw
where I've already made him soft.

"You lie still, my name sticky
on the sheet, and watch his hands stray
past ribs fanned with my sweat.
Faithfulness? A stream
that pulses through drought.
Or the delicate weight of your feet
on the bank, your forearm's arc
as you pointed to me,
knowing he had seen
and looked away.

"Like your shadow on the waves
I will vanish. And reappear
on infrequent days. You grip
your glass of water, suddenly afraid
of its simple taste, your fingers
like a child's, foreshortened and pink.
I'm not yours to hoard anymore,
your quickly drying stain.

You gave him what you thirsted for
and your tongue sweeps his lips for my flavor
of salt and reeds. Your skin,
a surface of blossoms,
hides the current we share beneath.

"Did you want that pull to take him
while he turned in my arms?
To wake him to your sway? He quivers
in your hands, tall and clear: now drink."

      3

In the overlapped shadows
of his body and mine, I reach out
for his muscled thigh, his fingers
which once brushed her waist
now smoothing my skin, gripping
my black hairs—he must close his eyes.
And lie back, the air between us
acute with sadness, as he waits for my body
to cover his, to admit his interrupted
tenderness. His legs wrap my waist,
ankles hooked at the small of my back.
Our fingers part my labia,
guiding him in, our mouths
rounding, every pore in the skin
saying oh. He grimaces,
his daily smile disappears
with each lunge of the hips,
my head thrown back. Her face shimmers
before me, then is gone,
and I draw away like an inlet of water

pulling my cold salt weight
from his sand with a sucking sound,
fingers sweeping his shoulders
sharp as rocks. He tosses his head
to be named and named, a shoreline poised
and overrun. A wind arches
through one body, the other.
His hazel skin against the pillow.
Then I can't turn away from his look
on my lips, breasts, exact as a rope on
my thighs, and hope for a shadow
to twist like a net between us,
crisscross my bare skin.
Her murmur begins: This close
you will lose yourself. . . .
I shake my dark curls.
My unseen muscles, pulsing,
hold to their taking.
The empty air
rises from our joined hips,
along our slick torsos, a triangle
opening.

Black Sky

He stroked her quickly, his satisfaction
only in a finished task. His beard
grazed her neck, his hand a distant
bird tiffling the leaves,
by habit skimming the shaved hedge.
Her untouchable
uterine bell her breath was reverberating he
didn't hear, too busy
working his way from breasts to groin.
His pleasure was the horizon
above the hedge she
twisted to see before it dimmed—
his cheek the illuminated plain of some
half-moon—but he pulled down
the window shade, patted her flank,
and admired her long gluteal muscle
until he guessed she wouldn't complain when he slipped
from the sheets to wash off sweat and semen.
He preferred not to think about himself,
not the black sky stabbed with light
as he came,
that fraction of empty hemisphere
which nauseated him with despair.
He was used to tending the patch
between her limbs, fingering
what he knew he'd find. She said
It's all I have
and tilted like a tree that's too slow
to find the light. He bent in their doorway
as if looking for something lost,
hoping she wouldn't call him back.

Night Swimmer

They walked down the beach at the end of Mexico,
three dogs quiet behind them. The man's face
was calm in a bodega's light
like the face of a dog content
with his companion's pace. She had given up
wishing he would talk, lulled by the
rustling on sand, the smell of charcoal
and brine. He was too sad to
shoo the dogs away. His brow was shadowed,
a new moon. His hand cool as bamboo around hers.
Her hem teased her ankles, as in the breezy doorway
where at dusk she had watched a young man
dive into the sea. Up the beach, drinkers laughing,
rotting turtle meat. Their pace steadied in the dark
and the dogs didn't stop to bicker over discarded fish,
obedient to the man's regular step, and the woman leading
like a steady wife, her sandals
swinging from her free hand, her feet
grazing stones and seaweed. The warm briny moisture
occurred like pearls between her legs, smoothing
with each step. He didn't want to think of that.
A sound arose in her throat,
round as a lime, and she pointed to the man
stumbling from the waves. He wasn't
fair-haired like her husband, as she'd somehow
thought a night swimmer would be.
Black hair matted his forehead, his red shirt clung
to his nipples, streaked with sea wash and salt.
Her husband wheeled toward the dogs
and said nothing. The swimmer
held nothing in his hands.

He looked at her, his whole face gleaming,
and looked away.
The dogs had vanished, and the husband,
though he didn't know it, knew for the tenth,
the twentieth time that he would leave her.
The moment folded into her rib cage, one wave
folding the next down the beach.

Husbandry

He stood in the corner,
hand on his chest, and
watched her. A cracked-open
walnut, its shell he felt cutting
his lung. Where would he
call to her from. A liquor
would break from the hollow
encased by the nutmeat and burn
his voice if he —
held
her, couldn't hold
himself here anymore.

She stretched her hazel legs
across the green bed, openly
since he had left. She stroked the
moist-apple sheen of her skin,
slipped one finger in
to the split flesh.
In the corners of her room,
his absence, slit window screens
flapping. Fresh evening.
The long round of her finger.

His pelvis
tightened when she
turned her head.
He could not step.
His hand smoothed the
catch in his
breath where her name
kept splintering. Her frown
surrounded him, and he couldn't see
to find her limbs.

Or sense his palm
on his skin, the amber flesh
she was remembering,
his groin muscle pulsing
in the odd September heat.
A riffling like leaves
against almonds. Her hands
streaking the bitter honey
down her thighs.

The Gilt Collar

The wedding veil pinned his
groin to their bed.
He wrenched it upward.
A mesh collar
in the sunlight, it glittered
around his neck—
now he was free at the hips
to fuck. He wouldn't
with her, so did it matter with whom?
She hoped the woman only gleamed
at the center of her pelvis because
his blind cock sensed a gold coin there
and had to bore it through. For months
her thighs had flushed as if pricked
by copper wire, shame
at her frustration.
He'd held still as she looked at him,
laughing nervously, his muscled belly
so gauzy to her fingertips, his blond armor
unseen. Now he flicked his
wrists in the sunset that reached
his rented room, red-gold hairs
etching his arms like shaven brass,
his suit of mail transparent
at last.
Who was the man
she'd sensed trembling beneath,
a silken sheen passing over his body?
She folded her robe to her oval breasts
as if closing another woman's eyes.
Across the bay, he held
the woman's face, his throat
cinched with elastic and lace,
waiting for the only way
he could cry out.

After He Left Her

Another woman's cry, gleaming
and black on the turntable. Then quiet
like a pillow half-sensed during sleep
billowed around her. Her legs tingled as she
walked through the house —as if she were a girl
who'd ambled home late from school,
tar popping in the heat, cars and willows
sighing past her—

to find no one there, the white stove top
serene, blue flames tucked into their jets.
All the books had promised this calm
when her fate would show itself:
the fairy tale's satin pillow
delivering the king's ruby
to the peasant girl. She hadn't expected
to find it here alone, stretched

across the king-sized bed, fingering herself
as if turning a page. Two teenagers were kissing
on pay TV. The girl's blouse
eased off her shoulders: a flash
of breasts, and behind her patch of fur
lips and clitoris glimpsed—
Night after night she lay watching,
her cry of pleasure
arriving through tears, still an unexpected
treasure, a ruby in her throat.

The Airplane

roars over the men in the vacant lot clattering lumber,
the Chinese woman at six a.m.
flattening cans to cement, my fingers
awake at the vibrating shade —
and it hums that night over The Nicaragua
where I sit eating empanadas, crisp banana crust
splitting against my teeth and gooey cheese
filling my mouth, my tongue immersed
in warmth, then thrust into
this absence
you left me to taste. The silence reverberates
as in the pause before the junior high dance
when I knew that the guitar and bass would vibrate
through John DaRoza's chest into my hands:

too late for us to listen to this emptiness
which echoed for years under the clicking of your weights,
murmured in the story of the fire you told
and told, as if the quiet would incite flames.
The motors young men wrenched down our street
subsided, and in the silence
you thought about driving away, revving
the engine privately. At last you chose the rim
of her bare plate, her lace curtains separating
like any in the breeze. It's easier
than I ever wished to stand
alone and hear the fueled wind
disappear, its absence circling
my chest. I wanted your warm hand
here, where it resonates.

The Wish

He drifts, he's never let himself float
like this, intangible as a lily bed
as my fingers pass into his torso and grip his ribs—
my hand pulls away, and he's sealed again.
His rosy nipples, his chest hairs a blond net of moss
on the surface of the lake.
Now he lifts himself onto the shore
and I climb out to lie beside him. The water
has shown him how to look me in the face,
healed the red wounds like mouths along his ribs.
He is promising to love me again.
My kiss was like a faint lapping, my gaze
as abstaining as water. He's gone half a year.

In another year, he says, he will see me as I am.
I think of his fingertips on my skin, moistening
with a salt liquid he wouldn't taste
and I stand smiling
as if I were still his wife, as if the lakewater could lift
from the surface and thrash against the mud borders
the miles an ocean hits the sand.
The moon is out. He looks now at my earrings,
pearls he once closed in his hand.
Over his shoulder, the large white circle.
Its pull passes through his torso
and angles into my pelvis, traveling down my legs
into the hard ground.

The Rail

Knives in the kitchen, blades angled into the block, a wedding gift. He had left them here with the other things. Now his name in a woman's high-pitched voice sliced through the windowpane. She thrust her head into the night, the cool air lifting her hairs. A woman clung to the porch rail, too drunk to stand up. The woman stopped calling him, started to cry. Words filled the damp air, disappeared, one woman gripping the cold window ledge, the other holding onto the aluminum rail with both hands.

The wife wished she could slice away something between them. Or cut a lump of matter from the absent husband's body where something had collapsed like an unused muscle. No blade could locate the ridge in his brain where the lies curled inward years before they met. She looked up at the stars misted with the city's light, touched the window, felt the metal entering metal as she shut it. The woman wavered down the street. The husband wasn't coming back. Buses and cars kept sidling down the alley, unexpectedly steady, trailing routes she could take downtown and crosstown, passages as if left by a long breath, which she took now unobstructedly for the first time in months.

Single Woman

She stood in a patch of scrub
on a high plain. The ridged desert below
was stained the color of plums,
covered once by the sea.
Her eyes burned with salt
that had hovered a thousand years
and each breath heated the mark
in her lung, three inches long,
as exact to her as an empty crack
she could see in the sunken dirt.
A man had left it there, had reached
down her throat and with one finger
made a tally. The flesh
of her vagina like a salty fig
was hers even when she gave it.
This burning when she breathed
was what he would not take,
how he repeated his refusal.
Her toes clung to the cliff,
the cool, succulent leaves,
her dust-brown skin
taut across the bones.
Anyone could hear it in her voice —
the scar her speech had to travel across,
the way sound rose through her heels
as from a coughing in the earth.
Later, she would walk through the market,
two brown pears rolling in her basket,
the curve of her palms nudely
gripping the rim. She would open
her door. The sloped ceiling,
loyal, white. Cool pear juice
sluicing her throat. And not a witness.

Hit

A nervous man came to my door, hoping
I'd welcome him in.
He told me of the pain
impinging on him which pried
apart his jaw.
I showed him my bed
and lay next to him
as still as the gray curbs
the cars drove between.
Said I'd lived with a man who
beat down stray sparks
from our sheets, afraid of sudden flames.
The visitor listened
but his eyes kept following
the cars, the small hinge
he saw in the middle of the street getting battered
by the wheels, and it rattled,
the right-angled metal bolted to nothing.

His blue eyes twitched toward my face and
away, watery with the cold.
He started to talk, his hard legs
pinning mine. I kept on smoothing
the sheet. Years ago a child
much older than I
made me sit at her feet. In the chill
she watched the men tarring the roadway
and told me all the times
she'd been beaten. Now in the quiet
I waited for him to say it.
He said Take me — How do I take you
apart? He saw my small hand
sweeping ashes from the sheets.
He kept talking. His eyes were wet.
I kept watching.

Viscera

Black hair slicked
along the head.
One hand
raised to hail.
Bracelets, brass
keys. Cars click by—
adrenaline strands on the tongue.
The swerving.
Scarified line of blood
on the inner lip, memory
of pus. Still upright
on a paved hill
below the flat white houses.
My abdomen muscles
patterned like lizard skin
in the cold light.

Before dancing, survey the room
covertly. No one faces
another. The straightness
of my teeth is unequaled.
The wrist turns, whitens
silk. Creases in
crooks of elbows, armpits,
tightly sheathed the breasts
lilt out from the bone
and his cheek cuts into
her lips pulling taut.
The urge to bite and
acute emptiness of mouth.
Drums crack inside
the ear, inhalations
of sweat, wipe it down to the
hip, the blade
streaked with something pink.

If I had that knife I'd
slice the skin from clavicle
to pelvis, through the pubic mat,
quitting before the clitoris —
peel back the first cutaneous
layer and show these
stranded, perfectly firm
muscles. Glimpses of bone,
capillaries, the tissue wet
and still not slit. I'd say
if you must come in,
enter this.

III

Love Poem to the Printed Text

I loved you because you appeared to me privately,
always waiting between the covers,
filling the pages my thumb riffled.
After I shut my eyes, you billowed across a dark field
like a sheet slashed with hieroglyphs
which let through the starlight.
The royal ball, the fox-boy,
her foot sliding into the slipper—
these you only pretended to describe, distractions
from your own procession, as transparent as black lace.

I wanted to bite into you, as into a wafer
where the first words were written. I knew
you were a single scroll ripped apart.
A piece flew out of reach: It was the moon.
No one could explain why you kept returning, imprinting
white rectangles throughout the world: One pair of hands
        waited
to hold you again, make you whole.

At first you spoke of my sadness, and the emaciated man
on the New York corner, the red leaves scattering
the grass. You became a woman
twirling in veils and a sequined bodice
and in the snow by the window hunched a wolf
into which her figure dissolved.
Her shoulders sloped like the letter f, his black haunches bent
in a pair of g's. The stone walls went white
to the edges of the page.

Every day my eyes scan this snow.
A figure walks silently, looking to either side.
I can't see if it's a man or a woman. Black footprints extend
between two lines of poplars. I glimpse

your arched neck, your fingers entwined beneath mine.
The sunlight fades, but I keep writing in the dusk,
trying to cover this surface, its sudden
flatness, like a face turning away.

The Door to Her Writing Room

lies across crates,
a makeshift desk peeling blue paint
like a sky stained with a storm.
There is nothing to keep out
the wind. It riffles her paper.
I stand on tiptoe, palms pressed
to the empty doorframe.
The resistant molding
reassures me. My mother will smile
home from the store
to see my arms stuck out
like the top of a T,
shielding her stories from the breeze.
My fingers spread out against the wood,
mismatched like her letters,
and my shadow crosses the floor
like her hand across the page.

If I shivered in the aisles with her
remembering margarine and milk
no one would hear the skitter
across polished oak, no one's knees
papered as if kissed—
a page blows through my legs.
I bend to catch it and
she's back, grocery bags crinkling
down the hall. She stacks cans
of soup in the cupboard
as I pick up sheets from the dust,
listening for my name, my palms
smeared blue with ink, my mouth an O
almost filled with "Mom" and biting
into her unfinished words
I shred the paper from my teeth.
Her silence

in tatters on my shoulders:
"I love you." "I made this."
The burner clicks on. Her face
in the doorway, lined with anger
or reprieve, doesn't
come back—the wind instead.

                    *

In the kitchen, the broad shoulders
of a man. My husband is washing
china, tilting the smooth circles
in his hands. Lamplight streams
like lemon broth across each plate.
When they gleam in the rack,
the whole stack separated, complete,
he turns to me. I crumple
the paper to my chest.
He will stand in the doorway. His glance
is steady, as if he watches me
match the torn edges,
her longhand
jagged down the page.

The Ledger

Your veins beneath translucent skin—a needle might pierce them. Too sad to stay home, you might have to go to the institution where needles shine in rows. At my bedside instead, inhaling my breath like ether, you care for me.

You turn down the sheets, smooth, cool, and white, read fairy tales aloud: The queen edgy with rubies stares at the banquet, unable to eat. The ungrateful princess has run away. The princess's deer is hidden in a closet where he can't break anything or breathe — and tears wake on your cheeks. I am awake in the sheets. Listening, I read the pace of the print through your tongue, brain, the saltwater stains on your face. The sheets closet me.

You describe porcelain plates. China edged with gold. The parchment unrolls —

(you are older. Almost smaller than me. A gray ash tree that could topple, a split branch in the dust at our feet)

—and the wide antlers sway. A taut deerskin falls to the polished floor. Strips of venison, red with rivulets, hang from a skewer. The princess has returned from her journey. She must feast. Her throat stings with animal salt, she shrinks into skin and veins. Wakes to an empty hall, her flesh restored, wearing the queen's tiara.

You smooth the white sheet, bend over the window ledge. Carts piled with apples line the lane. Watching them leave, your speech still urgent, you imagine your death. The veins flex of their own impulse, strands of opal. The sun paces, travels, descends. This daughter so tired of charting its track . . .

The procession continues. Dust. Seasons. Appearing and fading in your eyes. A fringed blue-gray bough, you bend down. A shadow on my ledger. In the lateness, my own beside it, ripening.

For the Wordless Body

Mute
the muscle constricts with thirst.
The scent of citrus in the urine,
sugar leaking
into a film across the eyes.
Morning fills the windowpane,
a lit rectangle to be hungry in. I hurry
past buildings, counting out streets,
a self with words
and a hollowing silence of cells.

Language punctures
the skin.
Slimmer than a pen
the syringe shoots the insulin.
The sweetness of tangerines
lingers in the bloodstream. The injection
combusts it into strength and heat.

Body, christened again
you burn too well, flushed
as an infant and shaking for food.
A frantic mother, I bend to you.
At night I fake the bravado
of a teenage boy pinching
a girl's bare leg,
the needle poised above my thigh.
For years you absorbed what I fed you,
then denied.
Now you try to refuse
the sweet essence that keeps us alive.

So I am vigilant
for the sake of eyesight and limbs,
grateful to have seen this particular death
and to walk away. I forgive us
this defect, the first defection
to the dissolving silence
trailing me like a cloak.
It falls from my shoulders
when my arms rise, awkward
and bare, a child's A
against the light.

Diabetic, Testing Blood

A drop bursts from my fingertip
and beads the white
test strip. I wipe the red away,
watch the reagent deepen
lapis lazuli and emerald.
The more brilliant the colors,
the sweeter my blood.

Hours later, I hope the stain
of my evening sample will fade
to azure and sand beige
like a swatch of a girl's cotton
washed in a stream.
Instead, I glimpse the hem
of a lady's brocade, blue as nightfall

above a tall hedge. Beyond it, her unseen
damask of crimson covers my insides,
shimmering with sugar. She is weaving
my flesh into satin as rich
as syrup, until I'm pale,
worn thin. I wish I could
lay the whole dress on the bed,

begin with the embroidered wrists,
unravel it. A hundred pinholes
won't tear me open, and no wind will
shake this lining clean. Before sleep
I'll draw out another length
of glistening thread, its end
in this scarlet fabric still hidden.

The Tailor

Black ribbon in his book, the print curled like thread.
His hard fingertips smoothing the tangle at seams,
at night tracing the serifs of letters only the eyes can arrange.
He mended the frayed satin edge of my blanket
and when I cried for it to tickle,
tore the threads out again. All that's left to touch now
are his clothes hanging from the hangers.
I ride underground toward him, walled in by intricate graffiti,
maps of trains and islands shaking and blurred, into the Bronx.

Candy-lover, sucker on verses, moaning over the world,
its Cossacks torching the shule —
through his iron fire escape soot has blown for sixty years.
I stare at a plate of sliced egg, a tangle of red cabbage.
The century isn't finished yet,
dead Grandpa, your eye-flesh dispersed in the earth,
and these markings persist, the red point of my pencil
piercing the engineer's text for a living
and leaving its fabric, like yours, in strangers' hands.

Uncountable bodies were burned, and afterward you lived.
Did you give me one cell, imprinted like a foreign coin?
I can't read it. What do I do but this scrawling,
my small hands whisking through air,
shaping your body as if calling out a golem?
Let me inhale one of your sighs, your tears fallen
in the theatre, the armchair,
and retreat into pages as pale as eggshells,
tracing the letters only one of us can read.

The Weight Taker

Trellised steel, a cage,
its middle a hull that can rock
in the waves if the whole
rig falls, the young men crawling
blind inside —I have checked the weight
of each beam, pinned or swaying,
each cylinder before it fills
with oil. I unroll the skeletal tower
again, grainy and flat
on my desk. I have nothing left
to correct. In a photographed ocean,
valves will flood the legs until they sink,
the highest braces rise from the waterline
for air, and sea chests screen
the tanks from the dissolving joints
of a different rig. This one will land
on the black seabed and the jagged
graph of waves in a decade's
worst storm will not knock it down.

At noon, the ocean sweeps over the city
in droplets, drags the lunch bag
from my hands.
An old man in a fishing hat
keeps spearing aluminum cans
from trash, pausing to sniff
the salty, diesel breeze.
I wanted to stand and work
on the high deck of a rig
whose weight I'd checked, to forget
everything but winches and welds.
But I sit on this bench, reimagining
the calloused, rusting steel,
exploding sand, my hieroglyph of lengths

erased, my center of gravity
irrelevant as the sea when the drilling
begins. Fronds waver underwater, sticky,
yellow silt drifts through the green.
Gas enflames above, and I can't
·check the fumes, the leaking
joints, the iridescent fish.
I cross my arms against the
weight of what I can't predict.

Clouds fall apart, regather
and pass, shrouding my shoulders.
My hair drips, slick as steel.
I wait for my hour to end,
watching the gulls float through the plaza,
circling me, their white backs
sprayed with fine rain.

The Writing
(After a Painting by Paul Klee)

The writing stands on the horizon:
two rust-orange lines
and a vertical bar below.
A woman made of triangles,
her head a plate of hammered tin.
Two sparrows fly from her shoulder
like an equal sign
toward the antelopes.
Above the smallest one, a red ball floats
which shows that he's a boy.
The true antelope is poised
beside him, watching
the wind on the low grasses.
His back and head are crescent
deep-blue moons,
and lit like a planet
the cornucopia tilts beside him,
a stylized bowl holding
oranges, their stems erect.
Two vermillion sticks
equal the edge,
the unsaid.

The painting hung above my childhood bed,
quirky and spacious like arithmetic,
ciphering the world
into its first, unsayable shapes.
In the daytime it looked flatter
as I knelt inside the circles
on the rug, keeping quiet
so my mother could type
her quick black strokes.
I had to wait until night
to be read to.

I tucked the words into my lungs,
the wrought-iron letters
that fenced in the roaring Beast,
the Beauty who caressed his face.
They broke apart
when she left me in the dark
and veered into the sliced landscape
above my head.

Now I write. The words rise
like triangular kites
and flap in the November wind,
agitated wedges of light,
unreadable again.
The cuneiform shimmers
on the curved horizon
and still indents my lungs
with meanings that would collapse the space
between dirt and sky if I could scream them,
tearing the array of slate and amber fragments
which is this world. Caught in its edges
I keep still for one more instant,
trying to read.

About the Author

Lisa Bernstein is a technical editor, specializing in geotechnical and offshore engineering. Her interests in the arts are eclectic. She has begun to perform as a jazz singer and she has staged performances of her poetry, incorporating dance, live music, visual design, and taped voice, at the Lab and at the New Performance Gallery in San Francisco. Bernstein is a graduate of the University of California at Santa Cruz (B.A. 1978) and San Francisco State University (M.A. 1981). She was a founding editor of *Five Fingers Review* and received an Academy of American Poets prize in 1981. Her home is in San Francisco.

About the Book

The Transparent Body was composed by Kachergis Book Design on a Macintosh II and typeset on a Mergenthaler Linotronic 300 by Azalea Typography of Durham, North Carolina. The typeface, Palatino, was designed by Hermann Zapf. Since 1938 Hermann Zapf has designed 175 alphabets for hand composition, Linotype, photo-composition and digital laser systems. Palatino is based on Renaissance forms and was named after the Italian writing master Giovanbattista Palatino. It was introduced in 1949.

This book was designed by Kachergis Book Design of Pittsboro, North Carolina.

Wesleyan University Press, 1989